mother power

MOTHER POWER

An Hachette UK Company
www.hachette.co.uk

Vie Books, an imprint of Summersdale Publishers Ltd
Part of Octopus Publishing Group Limited
Carmelite House
50 Victoria Embankment
LONDON
EC4Y 0DZ
UK

www.summersdale.com

Printed and bound in Poland

ISBN: 978-1-80007-278-7

Substantial discounts on bulk quantities of Summersdale books are available to corporations, professional associations and other organizations. For details contact general enquiries: telephone: +44 (0) 1243 771107 or email: enquiries@summersdale.com.

mother power

A Feminist's Guide to Motherhood

- ⚡ TRUST YOUR GUT
- ⚡ LOOK AFTER YOU
- ⚡ DROP THE GUILT
- ⚡ STOP COMPARING YOURSELF

POPPY O'NEILL

For myself

CONTENTS

INTRODUCTION

Mothers are important – we are powerful, influential, creative, innovative and dynamic. But while we spend so much of our time ensuring our families are cared for, who is caring for us?

Mothers work tirelessly to keep the world turning, but the world often doesn't work for mothers. It is assumed that we will be there to pick up the slack, serve everyone's lunch and cater to everyone's needs but our own. In the west, women's rights have progressed hugely in the past 100 years, but it remains a fact that once you've become a mother, you are expected to put yourself last. This is so normalized and ingrained that many don't see it, and it's reinforced by everything around us; from adverts to government policy; from greetings cards to beauty products. A 2019 study found that mothers in adverts are still shown to use all their knowledge and skills caring for their family, rather than for personal or professional reasons; a trend that hasn't changed since the 1950s.

This image of how mothers are "supposed" to be is so ingrained that when a mother is powerful and advocates for herself, it jars with people. It will upset some. But if you are brave enough to claim your mother power, you will inspire many others. It will allow you to raise children who respect women and understand what it looks like to treat themselves with respect. Most importantly, it will help you create a life that brings you happiness, fulfillment and confidence.

Women's rights took a battering during the pandemic, with mothers at the sharp end shouldering the majority of childcare and home-schooling as well as paid and unpaid work commitments. Experts at the World Economic Forum estimate this has put women's rights back four decades globally. The time is now for mothers to insist on respect and power both in and outside the home.

Mother Power is for every mother. Whether your child is grown-up or not yet born, biologically yours or otherwise; we are united in the experience of being female and raising children in a world that often belittles our contributions and hard work. Using feminist ideas about motherhood, this book will challenge you to unpick the ways we're "supposed" to be and truly respect the unique human being you are.

A note on power

Power is a word that's often thrown around, whether it's the power to choose or things that supposedly "empower women", such as makeup or high heels. It's become a vague concept, often confused with confidence. Confidence is great, and feeling confident helps you access your power – but if you don't have any tangible power, or you don't know what to do with it, it's just a feeling. Power exists both within and outside of you.

Power

Noun

The capacity or ability to direct or influence the behaviour of others or the course of events.

Power isn't accepting your lot in life and finding a way to enjoy it. Power isn't making the best of things or fitting yourself around the workings of your family.

In its simplest form, power is about influence. The ability to speak up for yourself and have those around you listen and take notice. It's about being able to create your own choices, rather than choosing from a limited menu of bad choices, and being the main character in your own life.

How to use this book

This book can be read cover to cover or dipped into as you please. The chapters are divided into different themes, all of which include a mix of ideas, practical tips and advice on how to shift your thinking and implement **mother power** into your life. At the end of each chapter there's a summary to recap key points and ideas for further reading.

Now and then you'll be encouraged to jot down your thoughts in a journal, so keep one handy for these points, and for whenever you have any other thoughts you feel like writing down.

If there's someone in your life – like a partner, friend or family member – you think might benefit from the ideas in this book, why not show it to them as a way to start a conversation. Some of the ideas in this book might feel useful, some might bring up an emotional reaction and some might feel irrelevant to you. Take what feels helpful from the book and let the rest go.

CHAPTER ONE:

SELF-CARE

INTRODUCTION

When you become a mother, it's really easy to start putting yourself second. Despite our best-laid and most feminist plans, babies are born physically and emotionally reliant on their mothers. As a result of this, the habit of neglecting yourself in order to care for your child is formed early and hard to break.

Taking care of your physical, emotional, financial and intellectual needs and desires should not be a bonus you fit in after everyone else in the house is completely content. You don't always have to be at the back of the self-care queue.

Neglecting your needs leads to anger and resentment, especially if it falls to you to make sure everyone else is fed, entertained and getting enough sleep. Resentment is poisonous to relationships, making it impossible to truly connect with your children or partner. If you're feeling angry and resentful, your feelings are justified.

If you feel like it would be selfish to ask for more time, energy or resources to devote to yourself, it's time to acknowledge the fact that you are a human being and you matter just as much as any other member of your family. Your feelings matter. Your physical and mental health matter. That caring for yourself makes you a better, more energized mother and sets a good example to your children is an added extra. You deserve self-care simply because you exist.

Read on for advice on how to prioritize yourself, feel better and show your kids how women deserve to be treated.

One in four mothers surveyed by Ipsos said they had less than 10 minutes per day for self-care. Eighty-nine per cent said they think women's self-care is a sign of high self-esteem, and only two per cent think self-care is selfish.

WHAT DOES SELF-CARE MEAN FOR YOU NOW?

Before kids, meeting your own needs might not always have been easy, but it was a hell of a lot simpler. Even finding the time and headspace to figure out what those needs are feels like a bit of a luxury after having kids.

This is your cue to spend a bit of time thinking about yourself.

There are six main types of self-care:

Type of self-care	What it involves	Examples
Emotional	Performing activities that help you reflect upon your emotions	Therapy, journaling, creative art
Practical	Tasks that are essential in day-to-day life that prevent stressful situations arising	Creating a budget, organizing your wardrobe, doing your tax return
Physical	Activities that improve or maintain your physical health	Pilates, walking, getting enough sleep
Mental	Doing things that stimulate your mind	Reading, visiting a museum, puzzles
Social	Activities that strengthen relationships in your life	Meeting friends, being part of a club, taking time to talk on the phone
Spiritual	Activities that give you a connection to something bigger than yourself	Meditation, self-reflection, yoga

As you might have noticed, the boundaries between these different types of self-care can get blurred. Taking a yoga class can be physical, emotional and social self-care, for example.

Think about what you need to feel good in all these areas of your life, and jot down your ideas in a journal. How are you taking care of yourself already and what areas of your life do you need to dedicate more time to?

Self-care while caring for kids

It's become a cliché that mums of young kids can't go to the toilet without the baby, toddler and dog in tow. But it doesn't have to be this way!

As long as your child is safe, you can take care of your needs away from them, even if they don't like it. Your child, no matter how old they are, is allowed to experience uncomfortable feelings.

It helps to talk to your child – even if you think they're too young to understand – about where you're going and when you'll be back. Learning that mum goes away and always returns is an important developmental process and going for a quick wee without them is a safe, manageable way to kick it off.

Temporarily experiencing difficult emotions in a safe, loving environment where they are comforted will benefit your child in the long run, as well as strengthen their bond with other caregivers.

Of course, there are limits to this – for example, the age at which you feel comfortable leaving your child with a babysitter is hugely personal and not something to be rushed. It takes faith in your own judgement to strike a good balance between responding to your child's emotions, keeping them safe and taking care of yourself. If taking care of yourself looks like staying with your child, then go with your gut.

BANISH THE WORD SELFISH FROM YOUR VOCABULARY

When was it decided that putting yourself first was a negative thing? If you don't put yourself first, nobody else is going to. And yet, so many of us were told as children that it was our job to put other people first in order to be accepted.

Never sticking up for yourself for fear of inconveniencing someone else might feel like it will win you friends, but all it really gets you is trampled boundaries and resentment.

If you use the word selfish to describe yourself or anyone else, try adjusting the language you use:

~~I'm being so selfish~~ **I'm looking out for myself**

~~She's so selfish~~ **She's good at standing up for herself**

~~That was really selfish of you~~ **When you did that, I felt overlooked**

Meeting a friend for coffee instead of doing housework is ~~selfish~~ **healthy**

It would be ~~selfish~~ **fair to ask my partner to take on more childcare**

It might feel weird at first, but the words we use to describe ourselves and others have a big effect on our worldview. Slowly, the way you think about things will shift, and it will feel easier and more natural to prioritize yourself.

Caring for myself is not self-indulgence, it is self-preservation.

AUDRE LORDE

WHY PUTTING YOURSELF FIRST MAKES YOU A MORE CAPABLE MOTHER

Your children need you more than they need any other human being in the world. This can be a daunting prospect, and the way many women deal with it is by putting their own needs and wants to the bottom of the list.

But you need looking after too — adulthood and independence doesn't mean having no needs, it means you're in charge of getting your needs met. If you're not taking care of yourself, you're not taking care of the most important person in the universe (according to your child).

When you take time and make use of resources to care for yourself — whether that means getting childcare, juggling weekend lie-ins with a partner or taking time for yourself while your kids watch some TV — you are not only recharging your own batteries, you're giving them the gift of a well-rested, less stressed and happier mother.

Not only this, you're also setting a good example of how to successfully and healthily be an adult. But beyond these not inconsiderable benefits to your children, you deserve self-care simply because you are a human being.

Nurture your female friendships

Perhaps you have a wonderful partner who you love spending time with. Perhaps you have a bunch of funny, kind male friends. Even if these things are true, there is no substitute for good female friendships!

Nurturing your female friendships is a powerful feminist act. Even if you have a female partner, platonic relationships with other women are essential to your well-being as a mother. Find a circle of women you can laugh, cry and empathize with, who understand what motherhood is like and you can be your true self around.

Who has popped into your head when you read that? Text that friend right now and arrange to meet up.

It might take time to find your tribe, so don't worry if you haven't found a group of friends yet. It's much better to have one great friend than a handful of women you don't feel you quite fit in with. Be yourself, say no to what you don't want and yes to what you do, and your people will find you.

SCHEDULE IT IN

By now you'll hopefully have an idea of what you might want or need to do in order to care for yourself better. But when you look at your week, it might not be clear when exactly you're supposed to fit it in.

If you have free time, that's great – go ahead and schedule in some self-care right now.

If, on the other hand, it's not that simple, you'll need to find time. This might mean letting other obligations go, finding childcare or asking for support from your partner, family or friends. Remember how important you are and reach out to others so you can make self-care happen.

Be creative

Depending on your individual set-up, you might need to get creative in order to meet your needs and build a life that works better for you. When you're juggling caring for others, caring for yourself is rarely simple. Not all self-care needs to cost money, require formal childcare or even take up big chunks of time. Here are some tips for thinking outside the box:

⚡ Look for small pockets of time in your day – could you fit in a regular 5-minute stretch or a 15-minute nap?

⚡ Build habits of self-care, such as packing snacks and water for you, as well as your kids

⚡ Keep a journal close-by, or write in your phone's notes app, for safe, emotional venting while you're with your children

⚡ Use your early mornings and evenings to grab a bit of alone time while the children are asleep

⚡ Maximize your self-care with any props that will make your downtime more enjoyable – for example, a great pair of running socks will make your morning run more comfortable, or a bath pillow to support your neck while you soak in the tub

⚡ Make good choices – grab a book instead of doomscrolling

Doomscrolling

Noun

Also known as "doomsurfing", is the act of spending an excessive amount of time on your phone obsessively scrolling through negative news.

SPOTTING BURNOUT

Mother burnout is real! The work we do can be relentless and time for self-care isn't always available. What's more, when you're already on a low ebb, doing things that will improve your well-being actually tends to become more difficult and it can feel like just another thing you're failing at.

Here are some of the signs to look out for:

⚡ Escape fantasies

⚡ Resentment towards your children

⚡ A short fuse

⚡ Fatigue

⚡ Guilt

⚡ Never feeling good enough

If you recognize yourself in this list, there's no shame in it. The well-being of mothers is rarely prioritized in our society, and we're expected and encouraged to overextend ourselves and neglect our own needs. Take a deep breath and know that it doesn't have to be this way. Have a frank discussion with your support network (away from the children) about how you're feeling, even if you're not sure what the solution is. If you're concerned for your health, your doctor will be able to offer advice too.

Summing up

Taking care of yourself is hugely important, but it takes effort to ensure you're able to. Remember:

⚡ You have needs and wants that matter

⚡ Taking care of yourself is good for your kids

⚡ You deserve respect and self-care simply because you exist

⚡ You have to make time for self-care or it won't happen

⚡ Text your bestie

Read this: *The Self-Care Solution* by Julie Burton

A relatable book about the realities of self-care and motherhood, featuring the viewpoints of over a hundred mothers.

YOU
DESERVE
REST,
HAPPINESS
AND TIME TO
YOURSELF

CHAPTER TWO:

SELF-ESTEEM

INTRODUCTION

There is nothing wrong with you. Low self-esteem is a side effect of growing up in a world that's constantly criticizing and comparing women. It's certainly not a reflection of your worth as a person.

Self-esteem is at the heart of good mental health. When you have a strong sense of who you are and how you deserve to be treated you're able to trust in your own resilience to cope with whatever comes your way. With a stronger sense of self-esteem you are able to cultivate a generous inner voice that enables you to comfort yourself during tough times and forgive yourself for past mistakes – kind of like an inner mother-figure.

In short, growing your self-esteem is one of the wisest investments you'll ever make. In this chapter we'll look at the reasons why self-esteem can be difficult for mothers, as well as ways to help yours to flourish.

A Norwegian study of 85,000 mothers found that self-esteem decreased when children are aged between six months and three years, and that lower maternal self-esteem goes hand-in-hand with lower satisfaction in relationships.

LETTING GO OF WHAT MOTHERS ARE SUPPOSED TO BE LIKE

Do you have an idea in your head of how a mother is meant to be? Many of us put pressure on ourselves to fulfill a fantasy version of motherhood that's impossible to obtain.

Grab a journal and jot down all the ways you feel like you don't measure up — not just as a mother but in any context. Now, I want you to cut yourself some slack. You are a human being, not a machine. You exist for yourself, not for others — not even your children. Remind yourself that you're doing your best and that your best is good enough. On a new page, write a kind response to yourself, acknowledging all the challenges you face and all the things you love about yourself.

This voice that you use to write your response could be your own, or it sometimes helps to bring to mind someone you regard as wise and kind — a celebrity or friend perhaps — who exudes warmth and compassion.

LEARNING TO TAKE UP SPACE

If you've ever tried to push a pushchair down a busy high street, you'll know that many public spaces are not made with mothers in mind.

As women and mothers we're often made to feel like we're taking up too much space. There's the constant pressure to be physically slimmer that affects many women (and is brought into sharp relief during pregnancy), the figurative space we take up with our opinions and needs, and the literal space we take up with our kid's paraphernalia.

Did you know that you can take up as much literal and figurative space as you need? You're not here to make other people's lives easier at the expense of your own comfort.

Next time you're out in public, try a game of "Patriarchy Chicken". Like the old game of Chicken, it involves holding your nerve while your instincts are telling you to get out of the way. But while playing Patriarchy Chicken, it's not cars you're refusing to move out of the way for – it's men who are oblivious to the fact that you have just as much right as they do to take up space on the pavement or train platform.

It doesn't sound like much fun, but as an experiment in what happens when you don't shrink yourself physically for those who unconsciously expect you to, it's eye-opening. Plus, practising walking around like you deserve to take up space (because you do deserve it) makes it subtly easier to stand up for yourself in other situations.

Patriarchy

Noun

A system of society or government in which men hold the power and women are largely excluded from.

MODELLING HEALTHY SELF-ESTEEM FOR YOUR CHILDREN

The way you speak about and treat yourself in front of your children has a huge influence on their own sense of self-esteem. So, when you're around them, keep this in mind:

Do:

⚡ Be kind, respectful and patient with yourself

⚡ Try new things

⚡ Talk about the things you like about yourself

⚡ Talk about your feelings

⚡ Speak up for yourself and other people

⚡ Include your own needs and opinions in your decisions

Don't:

- ⚡ Talk negatively about your body

- ⚡ Criticize yourself

- ⚡ Accept less than you deserve

- ⚡ Accept disrespect

- ⚡ Squash down your emotions

- ⚡ Exclude yourself from fun and connection

The more time you spend consciously being kinder to yourself, the easier and more comfortable it will get and the more you'll find yourself doing it automatically.

Speaking up for yourself

There are times when we all need to speak up for ourselves. When facing criticism from a family member, a thorny issue at work or even just an assumption from a friend, many mothers struggle to find the confidence to assert ourselves verbally if it might lead to conflict.

Motherhood doesn't come with a manual, so lots of us feel a constant low-level suspicion that we're doing it wrong. This insecurity in our own instincts is a big drain on self-esteem and leads to a fear of speaking up for ourselves, and instead, we end up deferring to the opinions of others to define what's right for us and our children.

When you need to gather the courage to speak up for yourself, remember that you are the expert on yourself, and you are the one who knows your children best too. Not your mother, not your boss and not a stranger at the play park. You.

Even if other people don't agree with or understand your point of view, you still have a perfect right to hold it.

Each time a woman stands up for herself, without knowing it possibly, without claiming it, she stands up for all women.

MAYA ANGELOU

Loving your body

For many of us, love is a big word when it comes to our bodies. The pressure to be smaller, sexier, smoother begins insidiously and, because we're exposed to it very early on, it's thoroughly ingrained by the time we reach adulthood. Pregnancy, breastfeeding and the huge lifestyle changes that come with raising children can change your body in so many ways, it's no wonder we can feel alienated within our own skin sometimes.

So, think of it like this: love doesn't have to mean romance and beauty… it's about care and respect. Love your body in whichever way feels most comfortable to you. Love your body like you would love something precious, vulnerable and complex (because that is exactly what it is!). By that I mean accepting your body as it is, without expectations to be something it isn't.

The Male Gaze

A phrase coined by filmmaker Laura Mulvey, "the Male Gaze" is the theory that the majority of media is filmed or photographed as if being watched by a heterosexual man, and that women absorb this view of the world, colouring the way they experience their own appearance and that of other women.

SEXISM AND SELF-ESTEEM

Low self-esteem is not a personal failing. It is a by-product of existing in a society that, despite the progress we have made, still does not value girls, women or mothers as much as it does our male counterparts. It's a harsh reality for many women and girls that they've experienced judgement, rejection or worse when they've acted with confidence and assertiveness.

Whatever your experiences with sexism, it takes a lot of courage and self-reflection to resist absorbing the message that you're not good enough. Forgive yourself for the ways you hide your confidence or apologize for your assertiveness.

Know that you are powerful only up to a point. Your confidence alone cannot change the world, but you can shift how you think about yourself, regardless of what the patriarchy seems to think of you. Believe in yourself and be on your own side, always.

Internalized misogyny

Noun

Unconscious sexist beliefs women hold about themselves and other women.

STANDING UP FOR
YOUR HEALTH

As well as having to navigate a health system where much of the knowledge comes from research into male bodies, studies have shown that women's pain and symptoms are treated as less severe than men's in medical settings.

Women endure a large number of painful symptoms that are exclusive to their sex, such as injuries from childbirth, painful periods and endometriosis; as well as the physical tolls of caring for children and health conditions that affect mostly women, such as fibromyalgia. All too often they are not taken seriously and told it's just another part of being a woman they'll have to put up with.

You don't have to accept this — it takes determination, but there are things you can do to make yourself heard:

⚡ **Request a female doctor**

⚡ **Get clear on your boundaries (turn to Chapter 3 for more on boundaries)**

⚡ **Keep a diary of your symptoms**

⚡ **Ask for a second opinion**

⚡ **Keep speaking up**

YOU DESERVE HAPPINESS

You deserve happiness, even if...

You have low self-esteem

You're single

You've made mistakes

You don't love your body

You have trauma

You have high standards

You have upset someone

Your kids take a lot of your energy

You love being a mum

You don't love being a mum

You work outside the home

You work part-time

You don't do any paid work

You're a step-mum

You have a mental health condition

You have a disability

This isn't an exhaustive list. Whatever you believe stops you from deserving happiness, add it to the above.

Summing up

Self-esteem is essential for claiming your mother power, but it's not as easy as just thinking positive thoughts. Remember:

⚡ Your self-esteem is a product of your environment, not a personal failing

⚡ You're fine as you are

⚡ Let go of impossible expectations

⚡ Care for your body

⚡ Work on your internalized misogyny

Read this: *Untamed* by Glennon Doyle

A rallying cry to women everywhere to start following our intuition and setting healthy boundaries.

YOU ARE DOING YOUR BEST AND IT IS ENOUGH

CHAPTER THREE:

BOUNDARIES

INTRODUCTION

Boundaries are essential. Far from being selfish, or a luxury, knowing how to say yes and no with confidence and without guilt is how you carve out a space for yourself in the world.

Your children need to know that you have boundaries in place to keep them safe, so they can feel free to explore, knowing you won't let them roam too far. They also need to be able to push up against those boundaries sometimes, challenging as those moments can be.

It takes practice to set firm boundaries, as our society discourages female assertiveness in myriad ways. Whether it's being guilt-tripped into sex, pressured into organizing the work Christmas party or calling a confident girl "bossy", women are trained to question their right to express themselves and set limits.

In this chapter we'll explore what boundaries are, as well as how to get comfortable setting them.

Boundaries

Noun

A personal boundary is where you draw a line between your thoughts, feelings and responsibilities and someone else's.

TOLERATING DISCOMFORT

From very early on, girls are taught in a hundred different ways that saying no and having limits is selfish and unfeminine, for example, being pressured into hugging relatives when we don't really want to. We carry these messages into adulthood, nestled deeply in our subconscious, and they manifest in many different ways, including impostor syndrome, people-pleasing and fear of success.

So, of course, setting boundaries is going to feel uncomfortable. It's going to feel risky, because your nervous system has been taught that setting boundaries risks negative consequences (for more on the nervous system, check out Chapter 4: Your emotions). Your inner critic probably has a field day when you set a boundary – with your kids, your partner, your family... anyone really. Putting yourself first is hard.

It's worth remembering that just because standing up for yourself feels uncomfortable and risky, that doesn't mean anything is actually wrong, or that you shouldn't do it — it actually means you're acting with courage. Developing skills to calm your body in these moments will help you act in your own best interests despite the fear you feel. Here's how to do it:

⚡ **Place one hand on your heart and one on your stomach**

⚡ **Breathe deeply so that the hand on your stomach moves**

⚡ **Think about your stomach, your hips and your feet. Bringing your awareness to these parts of your body helps ground you and sends signals of safety to your nervous system**

You might still feel scared, but hopefully a little less. If you have time, keep breathing like this until you feel completely calm. If you don't have time, just one conscious breath will help.

Setting boundaries with kids

Your mother power is never stronger than when you're setting a boundary. But standing firm with your children often comes with a generous side order of guilt. They want to stay at the playground for another hour, but it's time to go home; they want cake for breakfast, but you know they need something more nutritious. It can feel like parenting is largely made up of these moments and as mum, you're usually the bad guy having to enforce the boundary.

One thing that takes the pressure off everybody is to remember that kids don't have to like boundaries. It sucks enough that they have to leave the playground, it would doubly suck to insist they do so with a smile.

Try these tips when it's time to set a boundary:

Grant the wish in fantasy but not in reality:

"Wouldn't it be great if we could (for example) have cupcakes every morning? What colour sprinkles would you have?"

Respect their feelings:

"It's time to go. You might feel angry about it and that's OK."

Match their energy:

While staying calm, mirror their body language to show them that you understand how frustrating being a child is. For example, follow their disappointed sigh with one of your own and say "it *is* really disappointing. I get it."

Make a plan together:

"We can't do that today. Let's make a plan together for next time."

Offer future compromise:

"I really want that for you. Let's work out how we can make it happen."

Let them save face:

Don't make a big deal if they roll their eyes or have one more go on the slide.

TEXT YOUR BOUNDARY BUDDY

We're often least sure of ourselves when caught off guard. Just like you can come up with perfect, witty comebacks the day after an argument, setting a boundary when you're alone is a million times easier than doing it in the moment.

It's always OK to ask for some time to figure out your response when something is asked of you. This gives you an opportunity to check in with a boundary buddy.

A boundary buddy is a slightly cringy, made-up name for a friend you can rely on to remind you that you are entitled to set boundaries. They need to be someone you trust, and who thinks highly of you. It's likely you'll be your boundary buddy's boundary buddy, because we experience a lot less doubt when it comes to our friends' right to set boundaries than our own.

When you're unsure of how to respond, text your boundary buddy for reassurance – they'll let you know if you're being unreasonable, rude or selfish (spoiler alert: you're probably not being any of these things). Your boundary buddy will remind you of your power and send you on your way feeling confident enough to stand up for yourself.

Good enough reasons

If you're someone who says yes when you really, really want to say no, this is especially for you.

This tendency comes from a distorted idea of what counts as a "good enough" reason to say no. Good enough reasons might include:

⚡ Illness

⚡ Other plans

⚡ Childcare

⚡ Work

It's time to expand your list of good enough reasons to say no. You wanting a break, or having a date with a good book, or knowing from experience that the person asking will inevitably end up asking for more are good enough reasons. You simply not wanting to is a good enough reason!

When you know your limits and value your own well-being, saying no becomes easier and your life becomes less stressful.

Compassionate people ask for what they need. They say no when they need to, and when they say yes, they mean it.

BRENÉ BROWN

YOU ARE THE MAIN CHARACTER IN YOUR LIFE

Do you ever feel like you're a supporting character in someone else's story? Whether it's your kids', your partner's, or even your own parents', you feel like your life is arranged in order to make theirs run more smoothly. Even if you genuinely want to support them and their wins that benefit you too, this can lead to a small life lived in the gaps of someone else's schedule and needs. It's enough to make anyone resentful.

Carving out a story of your own needn't mean striking out alone or making huge changes. Start small – a good place to begin is to think about the things you loved doing as a child. Your ten-year-old self can offer some great insights into what brings you real joy in life, if you're willing to listen. Spend some time journaling on this subject and see what comes up. How could you rediscover those childhood pastimes?

Once you start doing small things that are just for you, your own boundaries, likes and dislikes will crystalize. Practise putting yourself first frequently. The more you do this, the stronger the habit becomes. Think of it like exercising a muscle – the more it's exercised the stronger it gets.

SEXUAL BOUNDARIES

Marriage and long-term partnership is hard. If you have a partner, finding time to connect sexually with them can feel all but impossible with children around. What if, when the opportunity arises, you're not in the mood?

Mismatched sexual appetites are common among couples, especially if childcare and housework isn't shared equally. Honest communication and the courage to have difficult conversations is the way to navigate this – as well as being aware of and confident about where your boundaries lie.

Boundaries around your body are one of your most basic and fundamental rights. Perhaps your partner would never cross your boundaries in this way, but if they do, it can be very uncomfortable to acknowledge. There are resources at the back of the book for support with sexual boundaries. In every situation and in every relationship, you have a right to sexual and bodily boundaries, always.

Setting sexual boundaries is about deciding what you are and are not comfortable with and communicating that to your partner. Of course, your partner gets to have boundaries too, and it's very normal for boundaries to change, even during intimacy. Establishing good communication is the basis for respecting each other's boundaries.

CONSENT ISN'T
JUST ABOUT SEX

Consent is needed for all sorts of things. Changes in the family's routine, big purchases and where to go on holiday require the adults in the relationship to have their say and come to an agreement they're comfortable with.

If you feel like your voice doesn't matter, don't stop using it. You are as much a part of your family as anyone else, and it's not OK for anyone – your partner, your kids' school, your family – to assume your point of view. If you're in the habit of going along with things, you might not get asked your opinion – give it anyway. Even if it complicates things or inconveniences someone.

Boundaries are ultimately about consent; what you will and won't accept, how you do and don't want to be treated. If you find people assuming these things about you – and getting it wrong – start practising the word no.

Finding your "hell no"

No is possibly the most important word in your vocabulary. As girls, women and mothers we're discouraged from saying no in myriad different ways. From housework, to unwanted sexual attention, to valuing our careers, exercising our right to say no when it upsets or inconveniences others is deeply frowned upon. Because of this, we have to work extra hard to get comfortable with saying no and holding firm when challenged.

Think about a time you said no recently. How did it feel? Were you challenged? What happened?

Your no is important. When someone pushes against it, it's usually a sign that you need to hold firm. When someone can't accept your no, it's about them, not you.

When it comes to your kids, you can coach them through accepting no – you can help them gain confidence in saying no, as well as accepting others saying it. Let them know it's OK for them to feel upset by your no. Help them understand your reasoning and offer compromise, but hold firm.

Show yourself the respect you deserve and treat your no as sacred.

... and your "hell yes"

We've covered no pretty thoroughly, so what about yes? Saying yes to what we do want can be just as difficult as saying no to what we don't. As mothers we often have to go without for practical reasons – from alcohol during pregnancy to sleep during the newborn phase – our own wants and needs get put to one side, over and over again.

Saying yes – to a job, coffee with a friend, a trip away – often comes with complications, childcare being the most obvious. It's often so much more straightforward to go without, say no, put it off until the children have left home.

You are worth the effort it takes to say yes. You deserve the support you so freely give to others.

What would you like to say yes to?

What would it take to say yes?

Summing up

Understanding your own boundaries and learning how to assert them is a process. The more you practise, the easier it gets. Remember:

⚡ You need boundaries in order to be yourself and look after yourself

⚡ Your partner, friends and family need to know your boundaries in order to be there for you

⚡ Your kids need boundaries in order to feel safe and secure

⚡ Practise, practise, practise

⚡ "I don't want to" is a good enough reason to say no

Read this: *The Life-Changing Magic of Not Giving a F*ck by Sarah Knight*

The boundaries bible, where the author invites you to let go of obligations and other people's opinions.

YOU BELONG
TO YOURSELF

CHAPTER FOUR:

YOUR EMOTIONS

INTRODUCTION

Motherhood is an emotional roller coaster. Loving another human being as much as you love your child is a supremely vulnerable act. Author Elizabeth Stone compares it to "your heart walking around outside your body."

Until you become a mother, it's impossible to appreciate just how emotionally challenging raising children is. Raising secure, resilient individuals without losing yourself in the process is a complex balancing act no parenting guide or friend can prepare you for. In this chapter you'll find ideas and advice on nurturing your own emotional well-being while navigating motherhood.

A 2017 study of mothers in England found that having a supportive group of friends had a positive effect on emotional well-being, self-esteem and feeling like a competent parent.

WHERE EMOTIONS COME FROM AND WHAT THEY'RE FOR

Emotions are mental and physical reactions that we experience in response to a stimulus. They are commonly accompanied by physiological changes in the body, such as crying when we are sad. There are five core emotions: fear, anger, joy, sadness and disgust.

We don't yet know precisely what emotions are, but we do know that they come about via our nervous systems – the complex web of nerves that links our brains to every part of our bodies. Our nervous systems pick up cues from our environment and feed them back to the brain. If, for example, we pick up on something that feels like a threat, the nervous system becomes activated. From this we experience fear and the urge to act to neutralize the threat. This worked for our ancestors when a sabre-tooth tiger wandered into their cave, and it works today when your kid's careering towards a busy road on their scooter. But the nervous system is also activated by social threats – the risk of being rejected or shamed – like when you set a boundary.

Our emotions are a source of information about how we're affected by our environment and how safe and secure we feel at any given moment. They're neither good nor bad; it's what we do with them that really matters.

What an activated nervous system feels like

Recognizing when your nervous system is activated will help you show yourself more compassion because it involves acknowledging that what is happening in your mind and body is a natural, protective response, rather than something wrong with you or proof you are in danger.

An activated nervous system feels like:

Panic	Fear	Dread
Tense muscles	The urge to run or hide	A loss of control
Shallow breathing	Increased heartbeat	Numbness
A sense of being overwhelmed	Chest pains	Feeling "out of your body"

These are signals from your body that try to tell you that you are in some form of danger. You might feel all of these things, or only a couple of them. If you can learn to recognize an activated nervous system, you're more able to calm yourself and assess how serious the danger is.

HOW TO TUNE IN
TO YOUR EMOTIONS

Emotions are actually pretty easy to avoid. Busyness, stress eating, housework, scrolling social media and focusing on other people are all very effective ways to dodge acknowledging and experiencing your feelings. The trouble with this approach is your emotions still want to be felt and expressed, and if they're not dealt with at the time they can come out in destructive ways – like passive-aggression and resentment – usually directed at the people closest to us.

If you're not used to tuning into your emotions, it might sound like a strange or complicated task. Here's a simple way of doing it:

⚡ Stop what you're doing

⚡ Take some deep breaths in and out

⚡ Relax by doing a body scan. Start at the top of your head and slowly scan your way downwards, taking notice of any physical sensations

⚡ When you are completely relaxed try to take note of any emotions you are feeling – there's no need to explain them, just recognize them

... And that's it. Once you've acknowledged your emotions, you don't necessarily have to do anything about them. Noticing is the first and most important step.

GOOD MOTHERS
FEEL ANGER

You are allowed to feel exactly how you feel. There are no emotions that are inappropriate or off-limits for mothers. Of course, the way we express them is important — but that goes for everyone. As mothers we're expected to suppress our feelings and needs, which is not only unhelpful but also incredibly unhealthy.

A simple way of treating yourself like your feelings matter (because they do) is by narrating them. Saying out loud, as calmly as you can, "I'm starting to feel angry, I need a minute," means you have the time to calm yourself and focus on the feeling you are experiencing. It also means that anger is less likely to spill out onto others and end up in you doing or saying something you later regret.

As an added bonus, when your kids see you taking a minute to calm down, they'll learn that it's something *they* can do too.

Processing emotions

What exactly does it mean to process an emotion? It's like any other kind of process – one step at a time.

Once you've identified how you're feeling, the next step is to allow yourself to feel it. Women are often labelled as over-emotional, so it's easy to get into the habit of dismissing your own feelings in the hope that they'll simply go away.

All human beings want to be seen, heard and understood. As adults, we can acknowledge and validate our own emotions. Even if your feelings of anger, fear or anxiety don't feel comfortable, acceptable or reasonable, they matter because you matter. Processing emotions doesn't always mean acting on them – often, our emotions aren't a sign that something is wrong, only that our sensitivity has been engaged in some way. When you allow yourself to experience your feelings, quite often, they'll rise like a wave, then disappear.

Other times, you'll want to express them more outwardly. Say you feel upset with your partner for giving the kids extra screen time. You can agree they deserve a treat while at the same time feeling angry that your rules for screen time have been broken and the boundaries changed. In this example, it's more about how you feel than what actually happened. Taking time to feel first puts you in a calm, clear place where you're able to articulate your point of view and tolerate hearing another's. Expressing your emotions in this way helps you and your partner understand each other more deeply and strengthens your relationship.

I am angry.
We should all
be angry. Anger
has a long history
of bringing
about positive
change.

CHIMAMANDA NGOZI ADICHIE

EMOTIONS AND YOUR MENSTRUAL CYCLE

The outdated idea that women are irrational and over-emotional is thankfully becoming less and less mainstream. Historically, this stereotype was based on the fact that we have cyclical hormonal systems. The menstrual cycle causes fluctuations in estrogen, which has an effect on our emotions.

Just because you have a menstrual cycle doesn't mean your emotions matter less. For around 40 years of our lives, most women are at some point in a menstrual cycle (unless we're pregnant or on hormonal birth control, which can also affect emotions), and this has been used as an excuse to dismiss and exclude us from power and decision-making. We make up 50 per cent of humanity, and our bodies are not a problem or a syndrome to be fixed.

The fact we have a working week built to suit a linear hormonal system shows just how much of the way we live is designed for the benefit of men. Men can act with all the emotional intensity of day 28 of the menstrual cycle every day of the month, and their emotions and opinions will be treated with respect and seen as normal.

Your menstrual cycle is not a reason for you or anybody else to diminish your power. Tracking and being aware of your menstrual cycle can be a tool for understanding your emotions, appreciating your shifting strengths and caring for your body effectively – in this way, it is a rich source of power.

What would you do if your feelings mattered?

You need to act as if your feelings matter, because they do. Can you picture someone with really amazing self-esteem, great boundaries and who respects both herself and those around her with ease? It might be a celebrity, a friend or an imaginary person that pops into your mind. She's your role model. Ask yourself: what would she do? When you ask yourself this, what you're really asking is: what would *I* do if my feelings mattered? Chances are the answer will be obvious, but there are usually barriers in the way; the fear of inconveniencing someone, what other people might think, anxiety about being unreasonable, or selfish, or unlikeable.

Your task is to do exactly what your role model would do. Start small – perhaps you have a free hour and need to decide how to fill it. How would your role model fill it? What's stopping you from doing the same?

The more you act as if your feelings matter, the more you'll experience how much better life is when you honour them.

SOCIAL MEDIA

Human beings are taking in information on a scale never before experienced, thanks to social media. Just scrolling casually through Instagram exposes your brain to the opinions and emotions of hundreds of people in quick succession, and that's before you post any of your own content for others to react to. This is going to have an effect on your emotions and self-esteem.

If you enjoy social media or use it for work, make sure it's a place that has a positive effect on how you feel. Be liberal, unapologetic and guilt-free with your unfollowing, muting and blocking. Whether it's a parenting influencer who makes you feel inadequate, a sexist comedian or a friend sharing conspiracy theories, you don't need that on your timeline. Many social media platforms also show you content from people you don't follow – if it's not the kind of thing you want to see, you can block any account you like, even if they're just a bit irritating.

Curate your feed so that you're not confronted with content that makes you feel afraid, ashamed or threatened as soon as you open an app. Research is beginning to show the scale of social media's negative effect on the emotional health of its users.

One German study found that reducing smartphone use by just one hour per day has benefits for mental health and well-being. Strong social media boundaries are one of the most important acts of self-care in the twenty-first century.

WHEN YOU'RE TRIGGERED BY YOUR CHILDREN

Kids are emotionally triggering. Because your bond together is so deep, their emotions and behaviour will inevitably raise strong emotions in you.

Many of us were brought up to believe that children's behaviour was something to be corrected and that displays of emotion were a problem. It's really important to recognize that, when your child's upset or having a tantrum and you're stressed out by it, you are both simply human beings experiencing emotions. Your stress isn't any more or less important, valid or real than your child's sadness or anger. The only difference is, you're the adult.

As the adult in the situation, it's your job to help your child move through their emotions, but it's almost impossible to do this when you're emotionally overwhelmed yourself. You know the saying "Put your own oxygen mask on first"? It means you can't help others until you've made sure you're OK first – that works for emotions too. So, in the heat of a tantrum, here's what you can do:

⚡ Ensure that your child is physically safe

⚡ Remember that your child is safe to feel this emotion

⚡ Take a moment to breathe deeply and name your emotions – "I'm feeling overwhelmed/angry/ashamed"

⚡ Once you feel calm enough, you can help your child with their emotions (more on these in the next chapter)

Naming emotions helps to reduce their intensity, by creating mental distance between you and what you are feeling. When you put how you are feeling into words, your brain can understand an emotion as an experience you are having, rather than a sign of danger.

Move your body

When you need to process emotions in a hurry, movement is one of the simplest ways to express and move emotions through, and out of, your body. When we sing and dance, the movement and vibration has a soothing effect on the brain and nervous system, making it a fun and cathartic way to release anxiety or anger. Here are some ways to bring movement into your day.

⚡ Find time for a sing-along after a stressful day – perhaps on your drive home from work. The words and feel of the song are important – pick a song to match your emotional state rather than something soothing. The aim is to bring your emotions to the surface and release them.

⚡ Have a kitchen disco. If tensions are running high at home, rope everyone into a mandatory kitchen disco. Dancing will help everyone expend nervous energy and help bring you all into a more harmonious emotional state. After lightening the mood, it can also feel easier to talk about things that might have been simmering unsaid beforehand.

⚡ You could even try yogic chanting, which has similar benefits to singing and dancing. Different chants are practised at different pitches, which move through and affect our bodies in different ways. For example, "Aum" vibrates mainly in your upper chest and shoulders, making it a perfect chant for easing tension in this area. Check out YouTube for tips on how to do it.

WHAT TO DO IF YOU NEED EXTRA SUPPORT FOR YOUR MENTAL HEALTH

If you're struggling with your mental or emotional health, contact your doctor – they can refer you to counselling organizations that can help. If you can afford it, a private therapist will help you explore your feelings in a safe, supportive and healing environment.

As well as seeking professional support, talk to your loved ones about how you're feeling. It's OK not to be OK and those who love you will want to be there for you. Concentrate on building small acts of self-care into your day, even if it feels hard. With support, you can feel like yourself again.

Summing up

Emotions are a part of life for everybody and learning how to compassionately respond to our own feelings is a skill that will make you calmer and more resilient. Remember that:

⚡ Good mothers feel all the feelings

⚡ Your feelings make sense

⚡ Spending time tending to your emotions is important

⚡ Your feelings matter

⚡ If in doubt, dance

Read this: *True Refuge* by Tara Brach

A guide to mindfulness and meditation that uses Buddhist philosophy to put you in touch with your emotions.

YOU ARE **WONDERFUL** EXACTLY AS YOU ARE

CHAPTER FIVE:

YOUR CHILDREN'S EMOTIONS

INTRODUCTION

Your relationship with your children's emotions is unique. Striking a balance between taking care of, and being responsible for, your children's feelings, while simultaneously giving them the skills and guidance to build emotional resilience, takes creativity, nerve and a willingness to be imperfect.

The influence you have over your children's emotional intelligence and resilience is at the heart of your **mother power**. This is both a huge privilege and a huge responsibility, but the good news is, whatever mistakes you make – and you will make them – the way you respond is what's important.

In this chapter we'll look at shifting how we think about our children's emotions, how to deal with big emotional blow-outs and the habits that grow emotional intelligence and strong bonds between you and your child.

A study of 53 Portuguese families found that healthy emotional attachment to both parents led to better emotional regulation skills for children.

ALL EMOTIONS ARE OK

It's really hard to see your kids hurt, upset or angry, and it's natural to want to make it all better for them. But when we don't allow our children to feel difficult emotions, they don't learn to tolerate or stay with their feelings. Being able to feel sad when something sad happens – without panicking or trying to squash down that emotion – is a valuable life skill.

Emotions will hang around until they're fully felt. So, if your child feels angry, it's going to come out one way or another. If they swallow down the initial anger, it'll often find a release, most commonly when a seemingly minor upset happens.

Children aren't always aware of where their emotions come from. They subconsciously pick up on emotional undercurrents and unspoken tensions within the family, but even when they can't articulate or understand what's wrong, their emotions still respond. As their mother, you are their safe place to express their emotions. If your children act out around you, this is a sign that they feel safe and secure with you – you're doing a good job.

WHAT YOUR CHILDREN NEED FROM YOU

In order to grow into resilient young people, your children need these things from you:

⚡ Love

⚡ Firm boundaries

⚡ Acceptance of their emotions

⚡ Reliability

Research has shown that children need just one consistent, caring adult in their lives in order to thrive emotionally. Every interaction between you and your child where they feel loved and understood goes into an emotional resilience bank. There are no grand gestures needed, it's consistency that counts.

Emotional resilience bank

The idea that when we have positive emotional experiences we top up our resilience reserves. The more we feel loved, accepted and understood, the more resilience we "bank", meaning when something challenging or upsetting happens, we have the strength to help us through the experience.

GOOD MOTHERS MESS UP

You're a human being, and you're going to make mistakes. On the previous page we talked about consistency, but consistency is a huge ask. Our lives as adults are not consistent, and it's impossible not to be emotionally impacted by everyday challenges.

When we do mess up — whether we shout at our kids, say Christmas is cancelled, or turn up late for school pick-up — it doesn't mean we're bad mothers. The important part comes when something's gone wrong and you need to repair things between you and your child. Far from being a sign of something terrible, this is actually a golden opportunity to deepen your relationship with your child.

Repairing goes like this: once you're both calm, bring up what happened. You apologize for your part in it and tell them how it felt for you. Finally, acknowledge how it might have felt for your child, and you listen to their point of view.

When you take the time to put things right, you show your child that their feelings matter. You might not get an apology or acknowledgement from your child for their part in things, and that's OK — it's a slow process. What's important is you setting an example to them of how to respond respectfully to difficult situations.

GOOD CHILDREN HAVE BIG EMOTIONS

Many adults encourage behaviours in children that make life easier for adults. Compliance, quietness, helpfulness and selflessness are some of the characteristics that are generally thought of as qualities of a "good" child. A "good" baby rarely cries and doesn't wake in the night.

But in adults, we admire and encourage assertiveness, confidence, boundaries and a strong sense of self.

Human beings don't get a personality transplant when they turn 18. If we aren't encouraging children to be confident and comfortable in their own skin and to listen to their own instincts, they won't turn into resilient, self-assured adults who can do these things.

Remember this next time your child asks you an awkward question, asks for extra ice cream, or says no to a hug from Grandpa. Raising a free-thinking, self-respecting human being who asks for what they need is a difficult job, and you're awesome at it.

Kids learn to treat others with empathy based on their experience of receiving empathy from us.

DR BECKY KENNEDY

How to talk to children about feelings

Talking about feelings doesn't come naturally to many of us; and even those who find it easy to talk to other adults about emotions can get stuck when it comes to children. It's like we believe that if we don't mention certain feelings, children won't experience them.

Talking about feelings doesn't cause those feelings – it simply brings them out into the open and removes any shame. Just like talking about difficult experiences doesn't make them worse. Talking about feelings is actually one of the best ways to process emotions and move on.

Here are some of the best ways to make talking about feelings easier:

⚡ Use playful, funny voices to lighten the mood

⚡ Talk while doing an activity together

⚡ Don't take it too seriously

⚡ Acknowledge the awkwardness

⚡ Be honest

⚡ Don't pressure them to reply

EMBODIMENT

Embodiment means using your body to show how you're feeling. When you embody an emotion, it's not the same as getting overwhelmed and taking it out on your child, it's more like playing a character – safe and playful. So, if you're feeling angry, act it out in as lighthearted a way as you can.

Stomp your feet and say "Argh! I feel angry that you're not ready for your bath!" You can then embody how you think your child is feeling by getting down to their level and saying "Argh! I'm having so much fun playing with my cars, of course I don't want to have a bath, baths are stinky!"

For teens, who might roll their eyes at this sort of behaviour, you can relate to them in a more grown-up way. Show that you take them seriously and understand them by subtly mirroring their body language and finding a way to meet them where they are emotionally. For example, if they're feeling left out of a friendship group you can sit with them, empathize and connect with a memory of how friendships felt for you at that age.

It might feel like making a game out of a situation like this will encourage your child to refuse a bath again and again, but what it really does is diffuse the situation by letting your child know that you understand and empathize with them. When they know this, the tension is taken out of bath time and there's less chance of another standoff next time.

DEALING WITH FEELINGS WITHOUT TALKING ABOUT FEELINGS

Sometimes, talking isn't what you or your child needs. Emotions exist beyond words – you can have emotional conversations with your children without saying a single word. This is especially true when your child is overwhelmed with emotion – a time when articulating their feelings and needs is often out of reach.

Here are some of the best ways to calm emotion without talking:

⚡ Bouncing: on a trampoline or jumping on the spot. For small children, picking them up and bobbing around works well.

⚡ Drumming: on your knees, a table, a tree…

⚡ Dancing: putting on some music and letting your bodies move in time with it is very effective for calming big emotions.

⚡ Walking: around the room, around the block… just get moving.

⚡ Humming: hum or sing a tune, or just a note. The vibrations in your vocal chords help calm body and mind.

These activities work to calm the brainstem – the part of our bodies that carries emotional signals between the brain and body. When your child's emotions are overwhelming them, talking won't do much because their thinking brains are "offline". Rhythmic movement will help their emotions become less intense so their thinking brains can function again.

PACE

When your child is overwhelmed with rage, don't try to overwhelm them right back with yours. PACE, a technique developed by psychologist Dr Dan Hughes, stands for Playfulness, Acceptance, Curiosity and Empathy, and is used by therapists to deal with emotions and conflict in a healthy, calm way.

Start by diffusing the situation: It's easier said than done, but if you can inject a little playfulness or comedy into a tense stand-off, nine times out of ten, you can diffuse it.

Follow up with acceptance: "You're feeling angry and that's OK. I love you."

Curiosity: "I wonder if you feel this way because..." (remember, you might be wrong!)

And finally, empathy: "It makes sense that you feel that way."

At any age, this routine will help your child feel safe and relaxed more quickly. You can save talking about any unacceptable behaviour until later – no one can learn when they're overwhelmed with emotion – and using PACE will help your child develop a healthy relationship with their emotional world.

Summing up

Learning to relax around your children's big emotions is a huge task, but one that will ultimately help them grow into emotionally intelligent, respectful young people. Remember:

⚡ You and your children will experience strong emotions

⚡ The magic is in the making up

⚡ Keep talking

⚡ Don't take it too seriously

⚡ You're doing great!

Read this: *The Book You Wish Your Parents Had Read* by Philippa Perry

Psychotherapist Philippa Perry explains the dos and don'ts of cultivating a good parent-child relationship.

YOU'VE
GOT THIS

CHAPTER SIX:

OTHER PEOPLE'S EMOTIONS

INTRODUCTION

We butt up against other people's emotions every day, in real life and online. People tend to feel a lot more comfortable sharing their emotions and opinions with women, and once you have children in tow, some take it as an open invitation to provide feedback on everything from your appearance to your children's behaviour.

Having other people's emotions put upon you can make you feel like they are then your problem to solve, which can cause a lot of anxiety. In this chapter we'll look at how and why we take other people's emotions to heart, how we relate to others and how to pick emotionally mature friends and partners.

A 2017 study of mothers and grandmothers in Wales found that pregnant women and new mothers experience more judgement and interference than they did a generation ago.

GENDER STEREOTYPES AND OTHER PEOPLE'S EMOTIONS

From very early on girls' emotions are treated as less important than boys. A study carried out by Sussex University showed that adults respond to babies' cries differently depending on their sex, with greater sympathy shown to boys.

Gender stereotyping is the cause of many of the ways women are on the back foot socially, psychologically and economically. One of the most common ways gender stereotypes manifest psychologically and emotionally in women is known as "people-pleasing".

People-pleasing

The emotional need to please others in order to feel safe.

If you're a people-pleaser, the prospect of conflict, being disliked or even disagreement can feel uncomfortable and sometimes even threatening. For people-pleasers, it seems like a better option just to go along with what other people think and want, even at the expense of their own needs. This disconnects us from what we truly think and want – we lose touch with ourselves by focusing on other people.

Gender stereotypes

Assumptions that are made about people based on their sex. Examples of gender stereotypes are:

Women are nurturing

Women are better at housework

Men are more sexual

Men are logical

Other people's emotions are nothing to do with you

The belief that we are responsible for the actions or emotions of other people is common among women. We're brought up to be nice and to put others' feelings ahead of our own. Becoming a mother can reinforce this because our children's emotions are, to a certain extent, tied to our own. As we're solely responsible for these tiny human beings for such a big proportion of the time, our own well-being feels like it's dependent on keeping them calm and happy.

The key to letting go of the idea that other people's emotions are our responsibility is to build a sense of trust. When you trust other adults to handle their own emotions and look after themselves, you can let go of some of that guilt that comes when you cancel plans, break bad news or give criticism.

What's more, when you hurt your own feelings in order to save someone else's, that's not actually you being kind – it's you trying to avoid your own discomfort. Many of us would much rather inconvenience ourselves than someone else, because the latter brings up complex feelings of guilt and shame that come from defying the stereotype of the selfless woman.

When you trust someone to deal with life like a grown-up, you're showing them – and yourself – respect.

GREEN FLAGS

We hear a lot about red flags for spotting people to avoid, but what about green flags that are signs of an emotionally mature person? Motherhood can be incredibly isolating, often reducing your social circle. With this new-found space for friends, keep your eyes peeled for people who:

⚡ Have close friendships with others

⚡ Give you the benefit of the doubt

⚡ Say "sorry" when they mess up or upset someone

⚡ Have some similar interests to you

⚡ Can handle being told no

⚡ Ask for what they need

What other people think of me is none of my business.

ELEANOR ROOSEVELT

WHY PEOPLE GIVE ADVICE AND HOW TO IGNORE IT

When people give advice, especially if it's unsolicited, most of the time they're talking about themselves.

Because every human in the world is unique, with a unique life, unique experiences, personality, strengths and weaknesses, the choices they make and how these choices turn out is also personal to them. So, when someone gives you advice – no matter how well-intentioned – they're talking to a past version of themselves. Either congratulating themselves on a good choice, or wishing they'd made a different one – it's all based on their own unique circumstances, not yours.

When you're on the receiving end of some advice you're unlikely to take, it's OK to ignore or decline it. Your own instincts are your best guide when it comes to parenting, work and life choices.

If you need to politely decline advice, here are some things you could say:

⚡ "It sounds like you did the right thing, that's really interesting. I'll think about that."

⚡ "That's a good point, but I prefer my way."

⚡ "Thank you, but I'm not actually looking for advice."

If these phrases annoy or upset the person you say them to, that's for them to deal with.

HOW TO BE THERE

When a friend is in need and you truly want to be there for them (out of love rather than obligation or guilt), it can be difficult to know what to do. If you often have the urge to fix or take on other people's problems, it can feel distressing when you don't know how to help. Simply being there is often what your friend most needs from you. Here are a few ways to truly show up for a friend in need:

⚡ Offer practical help

⚡ Check in with regular texts

⚡ Give a useful gift

⚡ Listen without judgement or fixing

⚡ Ask directly: How can I support you?

⚡ Take care of yourself

You are much better placed to be there for your friends, family and partner when you care for yourself first.

Unlearning people-pleasing

The first step to unlearning people-pleasing is to recognize it within yourself. If you:

⚡ Apologize often

⚡ Struggle to say no

⚡ Don't admit when your feelings are hurt

⚡ Often assume people are angry or disappointed with you

... you have people-pleasing tendencies. Once you can recognize people-pleasing in yourself, you have the power to take control. It's not easy, but it's worth the hard work. The secret is to learn to pause, name the feeling and breathe through the discomfort.

Saying no, talking about your feelings and resisting the urge to apologize will still feel uncomfortable. But armed with the knowledge of *why* you feel the urge to people-please, you'll have the power to choose differently.

WHAT YOU CAN AND CAN'T CONTROL

Other people's emotions are not within your control. Thank goodness they're not, because it would be exhausting if they were! Focusing on what you can control, rather than what you can't, can lead to better mental health and higher self-esteem.

Psychologists call the sense of how much power we have over our own lives a "locus of control". Everyone has a locus of control that falls somewhere on a spectrum between internal and external.

Internal locus of control: the belief that you have some power over the events in your life and the choices you make

External locus of control: the belief that events in your life and your responses to them are controlled exclusively by others

Of course, some things truly *are* out of our control, but the more we focus our attention on what we have the ability to change, the greater our sense of power, responsibility and safety in the world. For example, if it rains on your birthday you can't stop the weather, but you can dress in waterproofs or stay inside. Those who focus on the weather will feel worse than those who focus on how they'll adapt to the less-than-perfect conditions.

When you're feeling stressed out by other people, it can help to remind yourself of what you can and can't control. This diagram is a simple, all-purpose version, but you can create your own that's specific to any situation.

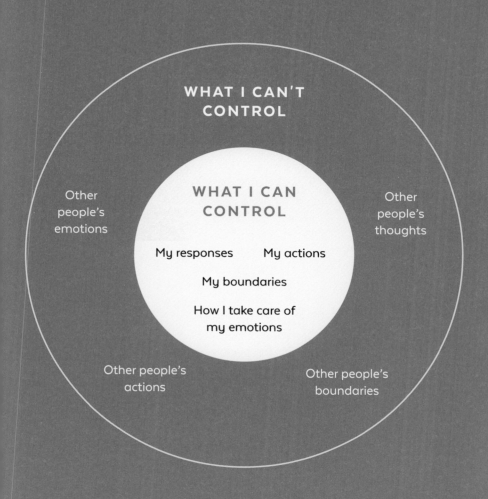

Your partner's emotions

If you live with a partner, theirs are the emotions that will most greatly affect you. This is partly because you spend the most time with them, but also because your attachment to them will most likely be the most emotionally intertwined.

Just like any other person, it's not your job to fix your partner's emotions. Because your partner's emotions feel so close, negative or heavy emotions can feel threatening or overwhelming to your nervous system. This is where learning to empathize and really listen comes into its own.

Empathy, in this context, means listening without slipping into problem-solving mode. It means validating feelings without necessarily agreeing with what your partner's saying.

Your partner might already have the skills to offer you the same empathy when you need support, but it doesn't always come naturally. Being clear about the type of support you want and discussing empathy when you're both calm will give you both a better chance of supporting each other when it's most important.

However, showing empathy is not the same as accepting disrespect. If your partner descends into name-calling, insults or threats during heated moments, it's best to disengage and return to the topic when your partner is calm and you feel safe and comfortable to do so.

Summing up

It's natural to care about what other people think of us and how they feel but putting other people's feelings above our own is a recipe for resentment and burnout. Remember:

⚡ Other people's emotions are not your responsibility

⚡ Ignore advice you feel doesn't apply to you

⚡ Gender-stereotyping is a trap

⚡ Please yourself first

⚡ You are admired much more than you think

Read this: *Playing Big* by Tara Mohr

A brilliant self-help book about finding confidence, courage and fulfilling your potential.

YOU ARE YOUR
**NUMBER ONE
PRIORITY**

CHAPTER SEVEN:

WORK

INTRODUCTION

When we say "work" what usually comes to mind is the paid kind, that you leave the house to do. But unpaid work is a part of the economy so much more than is acknowledged.

The world's economy is completely reliant on women's unpaid labour. On 24 October 1975, 90 per cent of women in Iceland went on strike for one day from all paid and unpaid work. The strike led to the Icelandic parliament passing a law equalizing pay the following year. It also paved the way for Vigdís Finnbogadóttir – a divorced single mother – to be elected president in 1980; the first woman in the world to be elected head of state. Today, Iceland is one of the fairest and least sexist societies on Earth.

Because women are expected to do everything – perfectly and without complaint – our contributions are only truly visible when they are withdrawn. In this chapter, we dive into the obstacles and inequalities women face in all types of work, and how to deal with them.

According to the UN, women carry out at least two and a half times more unpaid work than men globally. This unpaid work subsidizes world economies and government social care provision.

PAID AND UNPAID WORK

Work is work, whether you get paid for it or not. But much of the unpaid work — childcare, housework, household management — falls to women, even when we're in full-time employment. And because it's unpaid, it's treated like it doesn't count.

It's been estimated that if a stay-at-home mother were to be paid a salary for the unpaid work she does, she'd make over £100,000 (approx. US $115,000) per year. What's more, if it were a paying job, she'd get holiday, sick leave and her weekly hours would be capped by law.

Unpaid work is valuable, necessary and often hard. Whatever balance of paid and unpaid work you do, don't allow your contribution to your family to be downplayed.

Distributing work

Get a big piece of paper and a pen, sit down with your partner if you have one, and make a list of all the things that need to get done over the course of a month.

Include earning money, housework, childcare, plus any other responsibilities or non-negotiables you have.

Next, each choose tasks based on preference. Don't let gender roles guide you – keep going until everything is shared and you both do an amount that feels fair. If you're single, and if you can, work out which jobs you can pay someone else to do, get support from family or friends for, or even let go of altogether.

THE MOTHERHOOD PENALTY

The motherhood penalty is the pay gap between working mothers and similar women without dependent children. In the US and UK, it's estimated to be wider than the gender pay gap – and this is before you factor in the added costs of actually raising children.

Even more infuriatingly, there is no fatherhood penalty. In fact, fathers are paid an estimated 21 per cent *more* than similar men without dependent children.

The motherhood penalty exists because of the sexist assumption that mothers and pregnant women are less committed and less reliable than other types of employee. If you're discriminated against at work in this way, it's not you; it's structural and institutional sexism.

This isn't something that individual women can fix – it requires collective action. What you can do is call it out when you spot it. Look into supporting feminist organizations working to change society for the better, sign petitions, read up (there are lots of great books and resources at the back of this book) and write to your MP to get your voice heard.

WHY MOTHERHOOD MAKES YOU BETTER AT YOUR JOB

The motherhood penalty isn't just sexist, it's not based on any facts whatsoever. Motherhood gives you a whole host of transferable skills. Here are just a few of them:

- ⚡ **Time management: from fitting your life around a nap schedule**

- ⚡ **Communication skills: after acting as an interpreter, counsellor and teacher for your child**

- ⚡ **Problem solving: children are endlessly surprising and challenging, so you've learned to think on your feet**

- ⚡ **Multitasking: keeping several plates spinning is par for the course when you're looking after kids**

- ⚡ **Negotiation: not just any negotiation — negotiation with the most headstrong, unreasonable humans**

- ⚡ **Creative leadership: keeping kids calm and entertained during a traffic jam or wedding is no mean feat**

These might sound tongue-in-cheek but they're actually true. Motherhood will test your stamina, creativity and organizational skills like nothing else, and the skills you gain are invaluable in all sorts of situations.

Know your rights

If you're in paid work, it's important to know your rights as a parent. The company you work for might offer extras for parents, so be sure to check your contract and company policies. In the UK women are protected from discrimination under the Equality Act 2010, and in the US, under Title VII of the Equal Rights Act. It is useful to have these in place, but in practice many still suffer from maternity discrimination.

If you think you're being treated badly because you're a mother, there are lots of places to turn to for advice – check out the resources section at the back of this book to get you started.

There is no such thing as a woman who doesn't work. There is only a woman who isn't paid for her work.

CAROLINE CRIADO PEREZ

FINANCIAL FAIRNESS

Whatever your financial set-up, it's worth making sure you're getting a fair deal. If you're single, run your outgoings through a comparison website to see if you can get better value from your bills and look for the best savings rates if you have cash to spare.

If you're in a couple, any pensions, investments and capital should be shared in a way that feels fair and comfortable to you both, and you should both have a similar amount of disposable income. Recognizing the importance of your unpaid work is central to this, because the way in which you support your partner's career is a huge, but largely overlooked, aspect of household finances.

How capitalism screws us

We live in a capitalist society and as such, a lot of the respect and power society gives us is dependent on our ability to earn money. With women undertaking the majority of essential, unpaid work, the odds are greatly stacked against us, and mothers in particular.

While we'd like to think we've left the traditional housewife role in the past, women, on average, still do a staggering 60 per cent more unpaid work than men, while earning on average 15 per cent less per hour in paid work. So, women are still doing the lion's share of unpaid work, while doing paid work on top of that – thanks capitalism!

We're fed capitalist messages via advertising every day. We are constantly being encouraged to buy and consume more, compare ourselves to others and improve ourselves. One way you can start to disentangle your mind from capitalist thinking is to ask yourself often: who profits from this?

Try it next time you look in the mirror and feel ashamed, anxious or depressed about a part of your body. When you ask yourself this question, you quickly begin to see how advertisers exploit our insecurities and emotions in order to profit from them. The more you free yourself from these messages, the more your sense of self-worth will grow.

GUILT

"What we ask mothers to do is disappear and not make anyone feel awkward or uncomfortable."

British MP Stella Creasy on work and motherhood

Whichever way your life is organized, as a mother you're going to be criticized and expected to feel guilty about it. Whether we do full- or part-time paid work, volunteering or look after children full-time, the guilt and judgement we feel about it is real.

The guilt you feel is not indicative of your worth, it's the result of a system that is on one hand built to serve the needs of men with wives at home (and is largely hostile to working mothers), while on the other hand only values paid work and disregards unpaid work, despite it being essential to society and the economy.

In other words, you can't win, but you can let go of the guilt. Here are some strategies to help you:

⚡ Forgive yourself

⚡ Remember that there is no perfect solution because we are operating within an imperfect system

⚡ Strengthen your boundaries

⚡ Don't let paid or volunteer work creep into your free time or time with the kids, and vice-versa. Protect your time as much as you're able to

⚡ Be a "good enough" parent

⚡ If you can be emotionally present with your child and provide for their needs, you're doing enough. Let go of perfect and give yourself a break

Summing up

Work and money get more difficult to balance when you're raising kids, so it's wise to come up with a set-up that works for everybody in your family. Remember:

⚡ Unpaid work is work

⚡ The odds are stacked against you

⚡ Demand fairness

⚡ Resist capitalist thinking

⚡ Let go of guilt

Read this: *Pregnant then Screwed: The Truth about the Motherhood Penalty and How to Fix It by* Joeli Brearly

An exploration of modern motherhood with plenty of practical advice on navigating discrimination in the workplace.

ALL MOTHERS
WORK

CHAPTER EIGHT:

DELEGATION

INTRODUCTION

Sometimes, it all falls to you. This isn't fair, and it shouldn't be the case. Mothers deserve to be supported, but the way the nuclear family (parents and children living as a family unit) is set up relies on women always being available to take on responsibilities when the support system fails.

When your partner's ill, or the school's closed, or your carefully constructed childcare arrangements let you down, it falls to mothers to pick up the pieces, do the impossible, put themselves last and struggle through. The pandemic made it abundantly clear that mothers are expected to be the support system that cannot fail.

Short of a feminist revolution, we aren't able to change how society functions on our own. So, how can we arrange our own lives in such a way that we are supported where it matters, whatever happens? Keep reading to find out!

Outsourcing housework is a complex issue for feminists. Government schemes in Sweden and Belgium that subsidize hiring cleaners have helped reduce the gender pay gap, but critics argue they perpetuate gender norms because the majority of domestic workers involved in the scheme are female.

THE MENTAL LOAD

Ever had an offer of help but the effort involved in explaining how to do the helpful thing is so complex and time-consuming it's easier to just do it yourself? Say a friend offers to pick up some groceries for you, or your partner's taking the kids away for a night. There's so much information stored inside your brain that you need an A4 binder to explain your weekly food shop and a training presentation on how to get the youngest to go to sleep.

This is known as the "mental load" and it's like being the general manager of your own family. By being the main carer for your children, you've created and stored a vast amount of knowledge about the logistics, eccentricities and secret sauces involved in the smooth functioning of the family. The extra energy involved in passing on this knowledge becomes a barrier to delegating tasks and asking for help.

The way out of this is to trust your partner, or whoever it is who's going to help you. Yes, they might mess up. Yes, they might have questions, and yes, it might take a few goes. But holding the entire mental load is too much for any one person. Give someone else the need-to-know, take a deep breath and allow them the chance to learn on the job, just like you had to.

Expectations

So, you're ready to delegate to someone else. The reality of this is they probably won't do it like you do. It might take longer, it might look different, and it might not be perfect (but maybe neither is the way you do it!).

These are things you need to let go of. Yes, you have the most experience and are the most capable, but also you are a human being and only one human being at that. As long as everyone is safe and the tasks get done, you can allow other people to be less than perfect. And you can allow yourself to be less than perfect while you're at it.

Breathe, distract yourself, do what you need to do to tolerate any discomfort that comes up.

COMMON SKIVING TACTICS

If you're new to delegation and asking for support, your partner might be surprised or offended by it. Your ideas about how much is reasonable for you to take on don't come from nowhere. Stories, images and messages of women taking on every responsibility that is handed to them are *everywhere* – all you need to do is turn on the TV and watch adverts and popular TV shows to see how women are expected to take on the mother load.

So, you might encounter the following tactics often used to avoid taking on a fair share of the work, along with reasons why they're nonsense:

"I'm incapable because..."
These are obstacles that can be overcome

"But my mum did it"
All the more reason to set a feminist example to your own children

"Women are just better at this stuff"
This is pure, unfiltered sexism

"But I'm at work all week"
Unpaid work is still work

"I forgot"
Set an alarm on your phone

"The kids only want you"
That's because they've only ever had you – give them the opportunity to bond with your partner

STRATEGIC INCOMPETENCE

You might come across "strategic incompetence". This is when someone will perform a task badly, so that they aren't asked to do it again.

Dealing with strategic incompetence takes nerves of steel. If you can bear it, resist taking over, or even commenting, and allow them to continue. This is the extreme version of letting go of expectations from page 114. If the task they've messed up isn't something you can tolerate – call them out on it.

There is a delicate line to be trodden if you want to avoid taking back the mental load by spoon-feeding instructions. Suggest to your partner that they could try searching YouTube or Google for tutorials but do not take the task back. It's worth considering, especially if you have found yourself in a relationship where you are responsible for all the traditionally female unpaid work, that your partner genuinely believes that women are born good at tidying up and wiping babies' bottoms. Many men and women have been raised with these ideas. This is sexism. It's possible that it's not intentional – these stereotypes are fed to both boys and girls as we grow up – but this doesn't make it any more your job to teach them how to change a nappy. Open their mind by questioning the assumptions within your relationship.

HOW TO DELEGATE WITHOUT GUILT

The secret to letting go of the guilt you feel about delegation is to reframe the way you think about housework and childcare. Some things are your responsibility and some things are your partner's. Everything else is shared.

If you're the main carer for your children, that is your job for the time you are responsible for them. If you do paid work *and* you're the main carer for the children, that's two jobs you already have. Everything else — the housework, life admin, childcare when your partner isn't working — is a shared responsibility. Your partner is not helping *you*. There is a job to be done and someone needs to do it.

Just like it's impossible to babysit your own children, it's impossible to "help out" in your own house.

You are not a referee

When siblings argue, it can feel quite urgent to get them to stop. The sound of conflict between your children is emotionally stressful on so many levels, and as their mother it feels like it's your job to resolve the conflict and restore peace.

What's actually happening is your children are learning how to deal with conflict. If you're rushing to resolve it, you're teaching your children that ending a conflict is more important than speaking up for yourself, navigating through it and coming to an agreement. It's time to quit your job as argument referee and let your kids handle it.

If things are getting heated and there's physical violence or verbal cruelty, that's when to step in and help everybody cool down. But when it comes to talking it through and disagreeing, encourage your children to work things out between each other. It'll feel really uncomfortable at first, so take time to calm your nerves with some deep breaths or stretches.

Learning that healthy conflict is safe and essential for building relationships is at the heart of raising assertive, self-assured children, as well as unlearning people-pleasing habits within yourself.

Above all else, it is an act of immense generosity to be the architect of everyone else's well-being.

DEBORAH LEVY

WHAT COULD YOU LET GO OF?

Delegating jobs to other people is all well and good, but there are bound to be some things on your list that you could do without entirely. Unnecessary commitments become obligations and they bring stress and anxiety into your already busy life.

Is there an afterschool club, a voluntary role or a regular meet-up that brings you nothing but stress? What would it be like to simply... not do it anymore?

If all that's keeping that obligation on your list is guilt, consider this your permission to let it go.

Teamwork

When you learn to delegate and ask for support, you become part of a team. Even if you're doing the lion's share of parenting and earning, when you're part of a team you're able to identify where your weaknesses lie, and delegate jobs that you don't perform as well as others.

Your team extends way beyond your immediate family. If you're self-employed but hate paperwork, your accountant is on your team. If you're sporty but not particularly artistic, YouTube craft tutorials are on your team.

When you're part of a team, any problems that arise become a case of us vs. the problem, rather than you vs. the problem. You do not need to struggle by yourself, always ask for help with anything that's causing you problems.

Summing up

As mothers, we're often left unsupported, with a mountain of responsibilities to contend with. Figuring out what you can realistically delegate to others will free up your time and headspace. Remember:

⚡ You are not your partner's slave, PA or mother

⚡ Let people help you

⚡ Let things be imperfect

⚡ Let things go

⚡ Your team is bigger than you realize

Read this: *The Mental Load: A Feminist Comic* by Emma

Witty and effective feminist comic strips about modern womanhood.

YOU DO
ENOUGH

CHAPTER NINE:

COMPROMISE

INTRODUCTION

Holding fast to your feminist principles and demanding what you deserve are essential if we are to achieve female liberation from patriarchy. Unfortunately, we currently live within structures, such as government, education and social institutions, that we have little choice but to interact with, which are largely not feminist. We live in families with human beings who have their own unique worldviews and they won't always understand or be willing to follow your lead. Luckily, no one is measuring your feminist purity. You can have ideals *and* live comfortably with other humans who disagree with you in large and small ways.

What's important is to create a home, a family and a life that works for you just as much as it works for the other people in it. A life where you exist for you but also in collaboration with others. Yes, raising children requires sacrifice but it does not require sacrificing your happiness and sense of self. In this chapter, you'll find ideas on ways to collaborate with your support network to create a life that works for all.

A global study of parents and non-parents found what's been coined a "happiness gap". Research showed that in many nations people without children were happier than those with children. The researchers found that more generous government support for families means a smaller happiness gap.

FAMILY MEETINGS

Involving every member of the family in decision making sets a great example of respect, conflict management and listening. When children feel their point of view is heard and respected, they're more equipped to deal with change and challenges.

Here's how to hold a family meeting:

⚡ **Set the agenda** – be specific about what you're discussing and stick to it

⚡ **Take turns talking** – so everyone gets a say

⚡ **Include positives** – family meetings aren't just for crises, decisions like what to do at the weekend are perfect for a family meeting

⚡ **Take breaks** – especially if things get heated

⚡ **End the meeting with fun** – play a game or watch a show together

Compromise

It shouldn't always be you making compromises. Mothers are expected to be endlessly flexible so that no one else has to be, and just because you could, in theory, squeeze another errand into your day, make lunch for your partner or pick someone up from the airport, doesn't mean you have to.

Your happiness, time, mental health and comfort matter. Get in the habit of asking for compromise from employers, childcare providers and anyone else who asks you to make your life just that little bit less convenient.

Sure, sometimes they won't be able to give you a discount, a day off or a one-off favour, but getting in the habit of asking for flexibility from others, rather than only expecting it of yourself, will shift your sense of self-worth and serve as a regular reminder that you have a choice in every decision you make.

WHY COMPROMISING IS NOT PEOPLE-PLEASING

Where's the line between compromise and people-pleasing? The key is to ensure there's an element of give and take on all sides. Say the family car has packed up and you need a new one. You want something with plenty of boot space, while your partner's all about being eco-friendly. You'd look for a car that strikes a good balance between the two ideals, rather than prioritizing one over the other.

People-pleasing is about keeping quiet about your opinions and putting others' needs first. Compromise is about two or more people respectfully standing up for themselves until they find a solution everyone is comfortable with.

YOU WON'T ALWAYS GET WHAT YOU WANT

This is a difficult one, because you deserve the entire world and all the good things in it. But in real life, you won't always get what you want.

Sometimes you will get what you want, at someone else's expense, and that will probably feel horrible. Compromise isn't always possible, it's rarely neat and never perfect. Do what you need to take care of your emotions – even if you feel like you're overreacting.

You are the only person who can decide what you can and cannot live with. Disappointment is part of being human, but if a situation is still causing you anguish after attempting and failing to find a compromise, it's OK to revisit the subject.

Affirmations for discomfort

Standing up for yourself is uncomfortable. Women and especially mothers aren't used to it, so it takes practice and more than a little blind self-belief to do so. Remember: if you feel uncomfortable, this isn't necessarily a sign that something is wrong. It could just mean that you're doing something your mind and nervous system find risky. And as we've learned, the brain and nervous system think all sorts of feminist behaviours are risky.

When you feel the discomfort of insisting your voice be heard, try an affirmation. Affirmations work through repetition to get the brain used to believing positive things about ourselves. The more you think or say an affirmation, the easier it is for your brain to believe it. Here are some examples:

⚡ I am safe

⚡ I deserve to be heard

⚡ I am allowed

⚡ Just because I feel uncomfortable, doesn't mean I am in the wrong

⚡ Discomfort is a sign that I am being brave

Pick one of these to repeat to yourself or come up with some of your own. Affirmations are most effective if you practise saying them every day, so write them on Post-its and stick them somewhere you will see regularly, or save one as your phone wallpaper. Choose whatever combination of words work to tap into your self-belief and help you wait out the discomfort.

Love is a combination of care, commitment, knowledge, responsibility, respect and trust.

BELL HOOKS

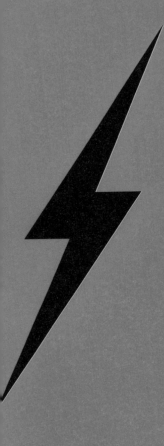

YOUR FEELINGS MATTER, EVEN IF THERE'S NO SOLUTION TO THE PROBLEM

Hands up if you've ever kept quiet about your feelings because there doesn't seem to be anything that can be done. Sharing feelings makes you vulnerable, and if it feels like it's pointless to do so, why bother putting yourself through that?

Your integrity, boundaries, opinions and emotions are worthy of attention, always. Even if nothing changes, even if nothing *can* change, even if you know it's for the best, you are allowed to have complex feelings and you deserve to express them. If nothing else, this gives your loved ones the opportunity to know and understand you better and strengthens your self-respect.

WHEN NOT TO COMPROMISE

Only you know what is and isn't worth compromising on. It comes down to your values – what do you hold sacred? It might be honesty, kindness, open-mindedness... but if you feel that you shouldn't budge, you must stand your ground.

Take a break and plan to revisit the subject at a later time. Keep talking until you've found a way forward you're comfortable with.

Abuse is one thing you do not need to compromise on. You never have to accept any kind of abuse in a relationship and you don't need to accept any responsibility for some else's abusive actions. Check out the resources at the end of the book for support with abusive relationships.

When you hit an impasse

Sometimes, a compromise can't be reached. Relationship researcher Dr John Gottman estimates that around two thirds of problems within relationships are not solvable. Two human beings with lives intertwined are bound to disagree on some things, whether it's politics, habits or something more abstract, like a way of thinking.

The important thing is not the problem, it's your choice whether to live with it. You are allowed to be your own person, distinct in many ways. By the same token, so is your partner and any member of your family.

Sometimes, you can't live with it. Be honest about this and proceed with great care and courage.

When you decide to live with the impasse, stop trying to solve it. The task now is to create a dialogue and boundaries within it. Accept yourself and your loved ones for who they are and assume the best, most generous explanation for their different viewpoint.

Summing up

Working together with those closest to you is essential for finding a way to live that respects everyone in the family. Remember:

⚡ Respect the voice of everyone in the family

⚡ You won't always get what you want

⚡ Always stick up for yourself

⚡ Compromise requires great care and respect

⚡ Your feelings matter

Read this: *Relationships* by The School of Life

A thoughtful, practical and philosophical guide to building healthy relationships.

YOU ARE
RESPECTFUL
AND YOU
DESERVE
RESPECT

CHAPTER TEN:

HEADSPACE

INTRODUCTION

In order to have power, you need to have headspace. Without space to think, to play and imagine, there is no way to create change and move toward a life that works for you. Without space to think about yourself and exercise your creativity, there is little chance to *be* yourself, and no space for power.

Feminism and female power has always originated in the minds of individual women and girls. *A Vindication on the Rights of Women* by Mary Wollstonecraft is regarded as one of the earliest works of feminist philosophy. Published in 1792, Wollstonecraft wrote: "Strengthen the female mind by enlarging it, and there will be an end to blind obedience." The "enlargement" of female minds depends on the health of our minds – the slow process of raising our own self-esteem, self-respect and self-love.

The 2021 Modern Family Index found that 86 per cent of mothers say the mental load for their family falls on their shoulders, taking up their headspace.

ACCESSING CREATIVITY

Creativity means letting your mind play. When your mind is relaxed and playful you have your best and most powerful ideas. Perhaps you already have a creative outlet in your life – if so, this is an invitation to dedicate more time to it than you currently do.

If not, you might think that you aren't a "creative type" – and you'd be wrong as we are all capable of it – it just comes more easily to some than others. Going for a walk without a set route engages your creative mind, as does playing with your children. Even meal-planning involves creativity (especially if you're missing something from the store cupboard!).

A 2020 study of Polish families found that when parents have time and space for creativity, it benefits their family relationships as well as boosting their children's creativity.

It can be difficult to know where to start, so here's a simple exercise to get you in touch with your creativity. All you need is paper and a pencil.

Hold the pencil in your hand and close your eyes. Scribble on the paper for a fraction of a second. Now, open your eyes – what can you see in your scribble? How could you turn it into a picture of something? Perhaps you could add eyes, legs or wings? Let go of any artistic expectations and just see what comes naturally.

Prioritize alone time

Time in your own company is essential for retaining headspace and good mental health. Mothering is a 24-hour job and no one can keep going without a break.

If time away from your children isn't always possible, there are other ways to snatch alone time and headspace.

⚡ Use screen time

⚡ Plan alone time during naps

⚡ If your child doesn't nap, introduce quiet time in a separate room

⚡ Listen to a podcast, guided meditation or music playlist

⚡ Get your child used to the idea of having 10 minutes of alone time

Needing time alone doesn't mean there's anything wrong (unless you've been deprived of it for too long). It's healthy to spend time apart from our loved ones, and your child will grow secure in the knowledge that you'll be back soon.

Headspace

Noun

The ability to think freely and calmly, without the stress of life getting in the way.

Rather than being taught to ask ourselves who we are, we are schooled to ask others. We are, in effect, trained to listen to others' versions of ourselves.

JULIA CAMERON

DEALING WITH JUDGEMENT

In dedicating time to yourself, standing up for yourself and claiming your power, people might judge you. Or even worse, your mind will fill up with the idea of people judging you, shrinking you back down before you even get started.

Know that you are your own biggest critic, and many of the judgements you feel from outside of you, in fact come from your own insecurities. Recognize that if and when others judge you, that is a reflection of them, not you. Remember when you were told as a child, that bullies pick on those they are jealous of? It's true, although by the time we reach adulthood that jealousy is usually buried under three feet of judgement. If another woman judges your choices and your power, it is because, deep down, she yearns to be powerful too. Shrug her off and wish her well.

SILENCING YOUR INNER CRITIC

You are your own biggest and harshest critic. It's easy to say "ignore your inner critic", but less easy to achieve this in practice. A better way of dealing with her is to get to know her, so you can recognize her voice.

Spend no more than 10 minutes listening to her, writing down her harshest judgements and cruellest jibes. When the time's up, take a look at what you've written and write a response from your kindest, most compassionate self to counteract the negativity. Scribble out the negative things you've written down or throw them away to rid yourself of them.

Then, when you hear your inner critic giving you a hard time for making a mistake or being a less than perfect mother, you'll know that this voice is not the real you, or the truth. Imagine you are turning a volume dial down on your inner critic, until you can't hear her anymore. Turn your kind and compassionate voice up instead and listen to her.

Therapy

Arguably, therapy should be available to everyone and not just a luxury for those who can afford it, but sadly it is out of reach for many. If you can afford it, it's worth considering. You don't have to be ill or even struggling with your mental health for therapy to be of use to you. Therapists are trained to be resilient, confidential, empathetic listeners who will help you to understand yourself and your emotions.

If talking therapy is not an option, there are other therapeutic activities that can benefit your mental health, including self-help books, talking to a willing friend about what's on your mind, ecotherapies, such as forest bathing and wild swimming, and alternative therapies such as yoga, massage and breathwork. All of these practices give you tools to calm and regulate your nervous system and bring a greater awareness to your mind and body.

JOURNALING

Writing in a journal works by drawing your thoughts out of your mind and putting them somewhere else. When a thought or memory is particularly troubling, our brains will keep it front and centre, trying to work out a solution (even if we know logically there isn't one). Writing these thoughts down helps alleviate some of the stress surrounding it by making it more concrete, as opposed to a free-floating anxiety.

A regular journaling habit provides you with a safe, judgement-free space to explore your thoughts and feelings, freeing up headspace for other things.

All you need is a dedicated notebook. You can write anything that's on your mind in a journal, but if you need a prompt to get you started, every day try writing at least one good thing about your day, and one thing you've found annoying or upsetting.

What do you want to fill your mind with?

Once you've created time and space in your mind, you get to choose what to fill it with. Be mindful and intentional about the media you consume, the things you spend your money on and the people around you.

Can you think of three things you'd like to stop allowing access to your headspace? It might be an account on social media, a judgemental friend or a conflict at work. How could you put boundaries in place to limit your exposure to these things?

Your mind is precious, powerful and full of potential. Fill it with things that nourish it, and you will feel your power grow.

Summing up

Having space and time to think and explore your own mind is how you build a life that works for you. Take the time to create headspace and be intentional about how you spend your time. Remember to:

⚡ Continue your creative journey

⚡ Make time to be alone

⚡ Let go of judgement

⚡ Find a therapeutic outlet

⚡ Fill your mind with good things

Read this: *Big Magic* by Elizabeth Gilbert

A playful and encouraging guide to aid creativity, even for those who don't think they're creative.

YOU ARE MORE
POWERFUL
THAN YOU
KNOW

FINAL WORD

"My home feels chaotic because the world is chaotic, not because I'm a bad mom."

Dr Pooja Lakshmin

Motherhood feels hard because it is hard. There is nothing wrong with you; the problem is that the world is built for men. Crash-test dummies are built using male measurements, meaning that women are 50 per cent more likely to get seriously injured in a car crash. Hundreds of thousands of girls and women with autism are going undiagnosed due to the assumption that autism is a "male condition". These are just a couple of examples that show us that women's lives are affected by sexism in many different ways and routinely overlooked in society.

Many feminists advocate for equality, but this can be an unsatisfying and short-sighted prospect. Even when 50 per cent of CEOs in the FTSE 100 are women, the baby will still need putting down for a nap. The plates will still need washing. Equality would require a separate group of people to do this necessary work, to make the world work for women as it does for men. The value we place on different types of work and different kinds of people is not fixed or natural – it's been invented by those in power to keep themselves there. The whole concept of power and value needs rebuilding.

Mothers are not just important, we are essential. We are important simply because we are human beings, and we're essential to our children. A mother is an integral part of a child's world. As mothers we wield huge amounts of power with the potential to influence the next generation. This is a huge responsibility. The way we allow mothers to work themselves into the ground, while calling it natural, is obscene. The attachment a child forms with their mother creates a blueprint for that child's mental, emotional and relational well-being for the rest of their life. As knowledge and awareness around mental health grows, the importance of mothers becomes ever more apparent.

There is a long way to go. Women are denied power in a million overt and covert ways in every country on Earth. To make the goals of the feminist movement possible, the struggle begins afresh in the heart, brain and body of every woman and girl. We need to reject the stories we've been told about ourselves that reinforce gender-stereotypes and exercise power over our own lives.

You are worthy of happiness and freedom, you have the power to create it – even if you don't yet know exactly how you want your life to look. When you start to realize your own power, there's a ripple effect. Once you find your voice, you'll find you influence people in a way you never knew you could. When you are honest, powerful and unwilling to accept less than you deserve, you grant every woman you encounter a magical, quiet permission to do the same. When you honour yourself first, you become more powerful than you can imagine.

RESOURCES

FURTHER READING

Reading feminist perspectives on motherhood, women's rights and parenting helps open our eyes to the ways in which women are affected by sexism in our society.

Chimamanda Ngozi Adichie, *We Should All Be Feminists* (2014)

Chimamanda Ngozi Adichie, *Dear Ijeawele: A Feminist Manifesto in Fifteen Suggestions* (2017)

Lundy Bancroft, *Why Does He Do That?* (2003)

Laura Bates, *Everyday Sexism* (2014)

Mary Beard, *Women and Power: A Manifesto* (2017)

Caroline Criado Perez, *Invisible Women* (2019)

Milli Hill, *Give Birth Like a Feminist* (2019)

Hollie McNish, *Nobody Told Me* (2016)

Adrienne Rich, *Of Woman Born* (2021)

Dr Jessica Taylor, *Why Women are Blamed for Everything* (2020)

Bethany Webster, *Discovering the Inner Mother* (2021)

ORGANIZATIONS

Pregnant Then Screwed – www.pregnantthenscrewed.com
Support and legal advice for women who have experienced maternity or pregnancy discrimination.

Maternal Mental Health Alliance – www.maternalmentalhealthalliance.org
Support for women's mental health during and after pregnancy and birth.

Rights of Women – www.rightsofwomen.org.uk
Free legal advice for women.

Gingerbread – www.gingerbread.org.uk
Charity supporting single parent families.

Turn2Us – www.turn2us.org.uk
Help with access to benefits, grants and support.

Birth Trauma Association – www.birthtraumaassociation.org.uk
Supporting women with traumatic childbirth experiences.

Relate – www.relate.org.uk
Relationship counselling and mediation services.

Gemma Women – www.gemmawomen.com
Digital courses dedicated to improving women's mental health.

Victim Focus – www.victimfocus.org.uk
Resources for victims of abuse, trauma and violence.

MASIC – www.masic.org.uk
Supporting women with childbirth injuries.

BPAS – www.bpas.org
Abortion services and advice.

The true extent of domestic abuse in modern relationships is impossible to know, but awareness and legislation around emotional, psychological, economic and coercive abuse is growing. Often, survivors of domestic abuse are not aware of how bad their situation is until they start to stand up for themselves. If you feel scared of speaking up for yourself because of how your partner might respond, it's worth contacting the following organizations for support, advice and guidance.

Women's Aid – www.womensaid.org.uk

Refuge – www.nationaldahelpline.org.uk
0808 200 247

Domestic Shelters – www.domesticshelters.org

NOTES

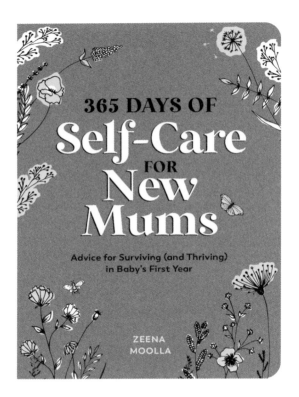

365 DAYS OF SELF-CARE FOR NEW MUMS

ZEENA MOOLLA

Paperback
ISBN: 978-1-80007-673-0

Motherhood is a magical experience, but it's also a time in your life that's emotionally charged and physically exhausting. Packed with tips and quotes, this book offers quick, simple ways to help you look after yourself. Because you deserve as much love and attention as you give.

Help Your Child Cope with
Change

What to Know, Say and Do
When Times Are Tough

Liat Hughes Joshi

HELP YOUR CHILD COPE WITH CHANGE

LIAT HUGHES JOSHI

Paperback
ISBN: 978-1-80007-194-0

As parents and carers, we try everything in our power to shield our children and prepare them emotionally for disappointments and upsets, but sometimes it can be hard to know what to do for the best. This book offers actionable tips that will give you and your child the tools to navigate these difficult times with kindness and care.

Have you enjoyed this book? If so, find us on Facebook at **Summersdale Publishers**, on Twitter at **@Summersdale** and on Instagram at **@summersdalebooks** and get in touch. We'd love to hear from you!

www.summersdale.com

IMAGE CREDITS